THE
Well-Ordered Family:

Wherein

The Duties of it's various Members as described and urged.

A small, but very comprehensive piece suitable to be in the Hand of every Householder; and may be especially reasonable in the present day.

Isaac Ambrose

Edited By:
Blair Radney

The Well-Ordered Family: By Isaac Ambrose

Copyright © 2017 by Blair Radney / Second Adam Publishing

All rights reserved.

Cover design by Blair Radney

Reprinted from the 1762 edition from S. Kneelan Queen-Street.

Editing of material was done to update the readability of the original text while preserving its character. These updates include minor grammar, spelling, and organization. To view its original source, a scanned copy can be found at www.digitalpuritan.net/isaac-ambrose/

Unless otherwise indicated, all Scripture quotations are from the ESV® Bible (The Holy Bible, English Standard Version®), copyright © 2001 by Crossway, a publishing ministry of Good News Publishers. Used by permission. All rights reserved.

No part of this book may be reproduced in any form or by any electronic or mechanical means including information storage and retrieval systems, without permission in writing from the editor.

For more books and information go to www.secondadampublishing.com

Printed in the United States of America

First Printing: January 2017
ISBN-13: 978-0692818619
10 9 8 7 6 5 4 3 2 1

CONTENTS

	Editors Notes	i
1	PREPARATION TO FAMILY DUTIES	1
2	DUTIES OF GOVERNOURS IN GENERAL	3
3	OF THE DUTIES OF PARENTS TO THEIR CHILDREN	9
4	OF THE DUTIES OF MASTERS TO SERVANTS	17
5	OF THE DUTIES OF HUSBAND AND WIFE	19
6	OF THE DUTIES OF CHILDREN TO PARENTS	29
7	OF THE DUTIES OF SERVANTS TO THEIR MASTERS	33
8	BIOGRAPHY OF ISSAC AMBROSE	37

EDITOR'S NOTES

There are hidden under the dust and yellowed pages of many books by godly men of the past, great nuggets of gold waiting discovery. However, most will never find them. This book is one of these gold nuggets. The difficulty of bringing these works to life in a modern age is due to the distance that has developed in grammar, writing style, and even the language over the centuries. Improving the reading enjoyment and benefit of this work took special effort to create a balance between preserving the original text and updating to a modern language.

To understand the difficulty of the original text, we must understand the writing style of the 17th-century Puritan. A popular style of the time was to create multiple layered outlines within large blocks of text. For the modern reader, it can be challenging to follow the author's thought as he jumps from one bullet point to another without clear delineation. In this edition, we broke the text into clear outlined sections which have been put into a traditional format to help the reader.

Other changes made include updating the spelling of words from old English, adjustments in punctuations, footnotes to give more insight into certain phrases, verses, words, or other items that were believed to be beneficial. Some items, however, were kept original; like the use of capitalization and italics. Phrasing or sentence structure was not changed to keep its original character. It's our intent these changes are faithful to the author, for both the reader new to the Puritan Classics and the purist alike.

May this work be a blessing to you and your family as you apply its simple truth in your relationships.

-Blair Radney

SECTION 1
OF THE PREPARATION TO FAMILY DUTIES

Now that we may more comfortably carry on these Family Duties, observed we, 1. Our Entrance into them, and 2. Our proceedings in them.

1. For Entrance, we must lay a good Foundation for Tractableness[1] unto Religion in those that belong to the Family. As, a. In the Governor. b. In the Governed.[2]
    a. In the Governor; the whose Duty it is,
        i. To endeavor in special Manner for Knowledge in God's Word; and for Holiness of Conversation in a Christian Walking. This would tend much to the preservation of his Authority; who otherwise will be slighted and disregarded, through an aptness in Inferiors to take occasion therefrom.
        ii. To marry in the Lord; and then to live chastely in wedlock, that there may be holy Seed: Now that he may marry in the Lord,
            1. Let Piety be the mover of his Affection; and Personage, Parentage, & Portion, be only as a comfortable accessary, considerable in a second

---

[1] The quality or state of willingly carrying out the wishes of others.

[2] Ambrose uses Governor and Governed to differentiate from the parent and child relationship. Emphasis is on the father's role and it was assumed that in certain understandings that the wife would also be considered the Governed.

Place: Christianity and Grace, is chief golden Link and noble Tie, which hath the Power and Privilege to make Marriage a lovely and everlasting bond.

2. Let him ply the Throne of Grace with fervency of Prayer: A good Wife is a more immediate Gift of God. Whence Solomon could say, *Houses and Riches are the Inheritance of Fathers; but a prudent Wife is from the Lord*.[3] Such a rare and precious Jewel is to be sued and sought for at God's Mercy Seat, with extraordinary Importance and Seal; and if she be procured at God's Hand by Prayer, he shall find a thousand Times more Sweetness and Comfort, then if she be cast on him by ordinary Providence.

3. Let him observe and mark these six points in his Choice: as, 1. The Report: 2. The Looks: 3. The Speech: 4. The Apparel: 5. The Companions: 6. The Education: These are like the Pulses; the show the fitness and goodliness of any Party with whom he ought to marry.

iii. To beware whom he admits to dwell with him, that they be tractable unto religious Courses. See David's Resolution herein: *Mine Eye shall be upon the faithful of the Lord, that they may dwell with me: He that walketh in a perfect Way shall serve me: He that worketh Deceit shall not dwell whithin my House: He that telleth Lies, shall not tarry in my Sight.*[4]

b. In the Governed; whose Duty it is both to join together in the Performance of *Family Duties* with their Governor, and to submit to his Government: *My son, hear the instruction of thy Father, and forsake not the Law of thy Mother; for they shall be an Ornament of Grace unto thy Head, and Chains about thy Neck.*[5]

These Preparatives I pin upon the Front or Porch of this Family: Now to the Family Duties themselves, and how they must be exercised.

---

[3] Quoted verse is Proverbs 19:14 apparently from the Authorized King James Version of 1611.

[4] Psalm 101:6-7.

[5] Proverb 1:8-9.

SECTION 2
OF THE DUTIES OF GOVERNOURS IN GENERAL

In the Proceedings of these *Family Duties*, we are to consider the Duties, 1. Of the Governors. 2. OF the Governed.

1. The Governors, if (as it is in Marriage) there be more than one; as first, the chief Governor, viz. the Husband: Secondly, the Helper[6], viz. the Wife; both of these owe Duties to their Families, and Duties to one another.
    a. That which in general they owe to the whole Family, is either, to their Bodies, or to their Souls.
        i. To their Bodies: Concerning which, says the Apostle, *He that provideth not for his own, and especially for those of his own house, he hath denied the Faith, and is worse than an Infidel.*[7] Now as the Spirit of God charges us with this Duty, so he sets us about such Things whereby this may be compassed; as,
            1. That everyone should have some honest and good Calling, and walk diligently in it: *Let him that stole, steal no more,* (says the Apostle, Eph. 4:28) *but rather let him labor, working with his Hands the Thing which is good.*
            2. That he bear a low Sail, and keep within Compass;

---

[6] Ambrose ties this relationship back to the garden where Eve is called a helpmate to the man. See Genesis 2:18.

[7] 1 Timothy 5:8.

remembering that of *Solomon*; *He that is despised, and hath a Servant, is better than he that honreth himself, and laketh Bread.*[8]

ii. To their Souls: Concerning which, some Duties, they are to perform to the Family; and other, to require of the Family.

    1. The *Duties* they must perform to them, are…

        a. To Provide that they may live under the public Ministry[9]; for otherwise how should they be brought into the Sheepfold of Christ, if they hear not the Voice of the chief Shepherd speaking unto them by these whom he has sent?

        b. To oversee the Ways of their Families; that they serve God: and as in all other Duties, to especially in sanctifying the Sabbath: To this they very Words in the fourth Commandment do bind all Matter of Families: *Remember, thou and thy Son, and Daughter, they Man-Servant, and thy Maids*;[10] Where the Lord speaks by Name to the Governors, as if he would make them Overseers of this Work of Sanctifying his Sabbaths.

        c. To set their House in order for the Service of God, to offer Prayers & raises to the Lord Morning and Evening. To this Purpose, *Pray continually* (says the Apostle) 1 Thess 5:17 which we must not understand of uninterrupted and incessant pouring out of Prayers, as the *Messalians* or *Euchite*[11] did; but of Morning and

---

[8] Proverbs 12:9.

[9] Ambrose is referring to the local church and its importance. Parents are to place the ones they are in authority over in it so they may listen to the preaching and instruction given.

[10] Deuteronomy 16:14.

[11] The Messalians and Euchites were a sect dating to the 370s who gave themselves to continual prayer, refusing to work, and begging for support. They were put down by Flavian, Bishop of Antioch in 376, condemned as heretical at the Synod of Side 388-390, as well as others councils in 431 and 426.

Evening Prayers; the Apostle here speaking in Reference and in Analogy to continual, or daily Sacrifices. This was *David's Practice, Evening and Morning, and at Noon will I pray and cry aloud, and he shall hear my Voice*, Psalm 55:17. And this *Job's* Practice, who sent for, and sanctified his Sons and Daughters; *and rose up early in the Morning, and offered Burnt-offerings according to the Number of them all: ---Thus did* Job *continually*, Job 1:5. And this was *Abraham's* Practice wherever he came, *to build an Altar to God*, where God should be worshiped jointly by him and his Family: *Gen* 12:7 & 13:4, & 21:33. And this was Christ's Practice for *himself and his family*, Mat 14:19 & *Job* 17:1.

   d. To instruct their Families privately in Matters of Religion, that they may not only profess, but feel the Power of Religion in their Lives and Conservations. This Duty has these Specials belonging to it.

      i. A familiar Catechizing of them in the Principles of Religion. Thus were Parents commanded of old; *Thou shalt teach these Words diligently unto thy Children, and shall talk of them when thou set in your house, and when thou walk by the Way, and when thou lie down, and when thou rises up*. Deut. 6:7. Prov. 22:6.

      ii. A daily reading of the Scriptures in their hearing, directing them to make Use of them: So *Timothy* was trained up by his Parents, and that *from his Childhood*, 1 Tim. 3:15.

      iii. A careful endeavoring that they may profit by public Ministry: To this end:

         1. They must prepare them to hear the Word, by considering God's Ordinances[12], Promises, and their own Necessities.

         2. They must remember them to look in

---

[12] These are the specific commandments of God relating to acts of worship and the sacraments such as baptism and the Lord's Supper.

the Word for a Christ, and for Communion with him.

3. They must examine them after the Ordinances, what they learned, and what Use they make of it: Thus Christ, after he had preached a Parable to his Disciples, he said unto them, *Know you not this Parable, and how then will you know all Parables?* And then he expounds the Parable to them. *Mark* 4:13.

2. The *Duties* they are to require of the Family, are both carefully to frequent the public Ministry[13], and diligently to be conversant in the private Worship of God, and constantly to practice all holy and Christian Duties comprised briefly in the Commandments of God; and they are to require these Things, not only by telling them, calling on them, catechizing them, admonishing them; but if they be negligent, by correcting them. Now this Correction must be ministered both in *Wisdom* and *Patience*.

   a. *In Wisdom*; whose Property it is to find out the right Party that committed the Fault, to consider of what Sort and Nature, the Fault is, to weigh Circumstances of Age, Discretion and Occasions; and to look to the Mind of the Doer, whether Negligence or mere Simplicity brought him to it.[14]

   b. *In Patience*: whose Property it is to make the Fault manifest to the Offender, that Conscience may be touched therewith; to hear what the Offender can say in his own Defense, and accordingly to allow or disallow; to avoid Bitterness, which sooner will harden the Heart, then reform the Manner of the Offender: These

---

[13] Ambrose is not talking specifically of the kind of ministry we often consider under taken by pastors and elders, rather he is speaking of the ministry that all Christians are called to perform publicly.

[14] Parents can often sin in correction by not exercising patience. Tiredness and frustration take over and result in over correction and a poor example of Christ.

Rules being observed and the Heart lifted up in Prayer to God for Direction and blessing, this Correction is necessary; as is evident in *Gen. 30:2*[15] *Prov. 13:24*[16], and *19:18*[17].

3. These are the *Duties* that *Governors* owe to their Families in respect of their Souls; to *correct them, catechize them, admonish them, call on them, read to them, pray for them,* &c. only with these Limitations.

    a. That they presume not above their Calling: This was Paul's Exhortation, That no Man take this Honor to himself, but he that is called of God, as was Aaron: The Honor here, is the Honor of the public Ministry; except that, and I know not but that every Governor of a Family, who has Special Abilities, Utterance, Memory, may read Scriptures, repeat Sermons, pray, teach and instruct out of the Scriptures. 1 Pet. 4:10.[18] Thus Jacob said to his Household, Put away the strange Gods that are among you. Gen. 35:2. And without all Contradiction (says the Apostle) *the less is blessed of the better*, Heb. 7:7. *And if the Woman would learn any Thing, let them ask their Husbands at Home*, 1 Cor. 14:35. Thus *Origen* would have the Word expounded in Christian Families[19]: and *Augustine* says, *That which the Preacher is in the Pulpit, the same is the Householder in the House.*

---

[15] "Jacob's anger was kindled against Rachel, and he said, "Am I in the place of God, who has withheld from you the fruit of the womb?" ESV.

[16] "Whoever spares the rod hates his son, but he who loves him is diligent to discipline him." ESV.

[17] "Discipline your son, for there is hope; do not set your heart on putting him to death." ESV.

[18] "As each has received a gift, use it to serve one another, as good stewards of God's varied grace:" ESV.

[19] Origen (184-253) an early Christian Theologian. The particular reference Ambrose is referring to is unknown, but Origen's early history included extensive theological training by his father Leonides which strongly impacted his life.

b. That they presume not above their Gifts: This was Paul's Exhortation to every Man, *Not to think of himself more highly then he ought to think; but to think soberly, as God hath dealt to every Man the Measure of Faith;*[20] yet I deny not but same Cases they may lawfully depute or substitute someone in the Family, whom they judge fittest unto Service and Employment, which they themselves should ordinarily perform: as in Cases of Old Age and weakness of Body: *Thus Samuel being old, made his sons Judges:*[21] Or in want of good Utterance or Expression of what is to be said: Thus Aaron was Moses his Spokesman[22], and stead of a Mouth: in in want of Boldness and Audacity, arising from a consciousness of Weakness: Thus the good Centurion sent Elders of the Jews to Christ to intercede for him:[23] or in Case that a Minister of the Gospel do sojourn in one's Family, as Archippus did in Philemon his House:[24] or in Case of necessary Absence: Thus the Apostle Paul made Timothy this Deputy to Christian Thessalonians: Or in Case the Lord has bestowed more of his Gifts and Graces to one than another: I known not in this Case, but that we may *covet earnestly the best Gifts in others, as well as in our own selves.*[25]

---

[20] Romans 12:7.

[21] 1 Samuel 8:1.

[22] Exodus 4:16, "He [Aaron] shall speak for you to the people, and he shall be your mouth." ESV.

[23] Luke 7:3, "When the centurion heard about Jesus, he sent to him elders of the Jews, asking him to come and heal his servant." ESV

[24] Philemon 1:2, and Colossians 4:17. Archippus was a minister of the gospel who Paul encouraged to , "complete the ministry you have received in the Lord." ESV.

[25] Appears to be derived from 1 Corinthians 12:31 (But covet earnestly the best gifts: and yet show I to you a more excellent way. – KJV).

SECTION 3
OF THE DUTIES OF PARENTS TO THEIR CHILDREN

The *Duties* in particular which *Governors* owe to the *Family*, according to their *Relations*, are either as Parents to their Children: or, as Master to their Servants.[26]

The *Duties* of *Parents* to their Children, are either to their Bodies, or to their Souls.
1. The *Duties* of Parents to the Bodies of their Children, are in many Particulars, but may be all comprised under this one Head, *A provident Care for their temporal Good*; and this extended itself to all Times, as 1. To their Infancy. 2. To their Youth. 3. To the Time of Parents Departure out of this World.
    a. The first Age of a Child is his Infancy, and the first part of its Infancy, is while it remains in the Mother's Womb. Here the *Duty* lies principally upon the Mother, to have a

---

[26] At the time of Ambrose, 17th century England, most households employed servants. This should not be confused with slavery, whereas servants were paid positions. There were many manuals produced during this time in the proper relationship between Master Servant, most equating the relationship as an extended member of the family. Today, we can gleam much from this as applicable in the employer employee relationship such as this from the 1664 book, *Advice of a Father, or Counsel to a Child* regarding servants; "*Be punctual likewise in their* [servants] *pay. When the work is done, the laborer is worthy of his hire; if he deserve better, encourage thy servant in well-doing; this will encourage him for the future to do well.*"

special Care of it, that it may be safely brought forth. Why was the Charge of *abstaining from Wine, strong Drinks, and unclean Things*, given to *Manoah's* Wife, but because *of the Child which she had conceived?*[27]

The next Degree of a Childs Infancy, is while it is in the Swadling-band[28], and remains a sucking child; in this also the Care more especially lies on the Mother, whose *Duty* it is to take all the pains she possibility may, for the Education of her Child; and especially to give her Child suck, if she be able thereto: This not only Nature, but Scripture sets forth;

i. By Consequence, *Gen.* 49:25[29], *Hos.* 9:14[30], *1 Tim.* 5:10[31].
ii. By Example, *Gen.* 21:7[32], *1 Sam.* 1:23[33], *Psalm* 22:9[34].
iii. By Grant, the Word giving it as a ruled Care not to be

---

[27] Judges 13:4, An angle appeared to Manoah's wife who was barren and promised a child. She was told to abstain from alcohol This child was Samson who would judge Israel probably around the 11th century BC.

[28] Swadling-bands were strips of cloth wrapped around an infant to restrict their movement. This was believed to keep them from injuring themselves and becoming deformed. This would be performed until the child was 8-9 months. The practice was falling out of favor during the time of Ambrose's writing.

[29] "…blessings of the breasts and of the womb" ESV.

[30] "…Give them a miscarrying womb and dry breasts. ESV.

[31] "And well reported of for good works: if she have nourished her children" Geneva bible translation.

[32] "Who would have said to Abraham that Sarah would nurse children?" ESV.

[33] "…So the woman remained and nursed her son until she weaned him." ESV.

[34] "…you made me trust you at my mother's breasts." ESV.

denied, *Gen.* 21:7, *Cant.* 8:1[35], *Luke* 11:27[36].

    b. The second Age of a Child is its Youth, from the Time it begins to be of any Discretion, till it be fit to be placed forth: Now the Duty of Parents at this Time is, 1. To nourish. 2. To nurture their Children.

        i. Under *Nourishment*, are comprised Food, Apparel, Recreation, Means for Recovery of Health when they are sick: In which, if Parents provide not for their Children, *they are worse than Infidels.*[37]

        ii. And under *Nourishment*, are comprised, good Manners, a good Calling, frequent Admonition, Reprehension, Correction, the last Remedy, which may do good when nothing else can. *Prov.* 19:18[38], 23:13, 14[39], 29:17[40].

    c. The last Time to which Parents provident Care extend it self, is the Time of their Departure out of the World; and then they are to set their House in Order, and to leave their estates to their Children.

2. The *Duty* of Parents to the *Souls* of their Children extends itself also to all Times: 1: To their Infancy 2. To their Youth. 3. To the Time of Parents Departure out of this World.

    a. The first Age of a Child, is his infancy: and the first Part of

---

[35] Canticle of Canticles or Song of Solomon. A canticle is a song of Hymn used regularly in the service of a church. The Song of Solomon is also referred to as the Canticle of Canticle as a place of honor. The tradition of this name goes back to the use of the Vulgate. "Oh that you were like a brother to me who nursed at my mother's breasts!" ESV

[36] "…Blessed is the womb that bore you, and the breasts at which you nursed!" ESV.

[37] 1 Tim. 5:8.

[38] "…Discipline your son, for there is hope; do not set your heart on putting him to death." ESV.

[39] "Do not withhold discipline from a child; if you strike him with a rod, he will not die"; "If you strike him with the rod, you will save his soul from Sheol."

[40] "Discipline your son, and he will give you rest; he will give delight to your heart."

its Infancy, is while is while it remains in the Mother's Womb. Now the Duty of the Parent at that Time are these:

i. That they pray for their Children: Thus did *Rebekah*[41], while the Children were quick in her womb. Those Parents that neglect this *Duty* to their Children, consider not rightly that they are conceived in Sin.

ii. That they make sure (so much as in them lies) that their Children be born under the Promise, or under the Covenant, in respect of the Spiritual Part of it: How? *By making sure that they be under the Promise or Covenant themselves*. If God in Christ be their God, they may have a comfortable Hope, that God will be the God of their Seed, according to the Promise, *I will be thy God, and the God of thy Seed*, Gen. 17:7.

The next Degree of a Child's Infancy, is when it is born: and the *Duty* of Parents then is, to give up their Children unto God, casting them into the Hands of his Providence, into the Arms of his Mercy, begging for them to the Ordinance, *the Sacrament of Baptism*[42], to get the Seal of the Covenant set upon them, to get them marked out for Salvation.

b. The second Age of a Child, is it's Youth: Now the *Duty* of Parents to their Children at this Time, is to train them up in true Piety: *To bring them up in the Nurture and Admonition of the Lord*.[43] To this end,

i. When Children begin to read, let them *read the holy Scriptures*: so was *Timothy trained up from a Child*;[44] and thus

---

[41] Gen. 25:21-23.

[42] Ambrose holds to a pedobaptism, the editor does not agree with this view. As a counterpoint the Baptist Confession of Faith of 1689 states in Chapter 29 paragraph 2 that, *"Those who do actually profess repentance towards God, faith in, and obedience to, our Lord Jesus Christ, are the only proper subjects of this ordinance."* See Mark 16:16, Acts 8:36, 37, 2:41, 8:12, and Acts 18:8. Parents instead should dedicate themselves to teaching them the way and need of salvation while relying on God's timing for salvation.

[43] Eph. 6:4b.

[44] 2 Timothy 3:15; "and how from childhood you have been acquainted with the

will Children suck in Religion with learning.

ii. Let Children be Catechized consistently from Day to Day; only with this Caveat, that Parents deal with their Children, as skillful Nurses and Mothers do in feeding their Children, not to give them too much at once: overmuch dulls a Child's Understanding, and breeds Wearisomeness to it; it is most suitable to give them *Precept up Precept, Precept upon Precept, Line upon Line, Line upon Line, here a little & there a little*, Isaiah 28:10. Thus shall they learn with Ease & Delight, and Time a great Measure of Knowledge will be gained thereby.

iii. Let Parents declare to their Children, the admirable Works that God in former Times hath done for his Church, especially such Works as he hath done in their Time: outward sensible Things do best work upon Children, and therefore this direction was given under the Law, *Job* 4:6, 21[45].

iv. Let Parents be to their Children a good Pattern in Piety, leading them to Christ by their Examples: This will take Place with Children, more than all Precepts or parental Instructions: *But as for me (said Joshua) and my House, we will serve the Lord*: Joshua 14:13. He sets himself first, as a Guide to the rest.

v. Let Parents reprove and correct their Children for Sin; and that the Lord may sanctify this Correction unto them; *Consider this, O ye Parents*, Do you observe such and such Sins in your Children? Enter into your own Hearts, examine yourselves, whether they come not from you: Consider, how justly the Hand of God may be upon you: and when you are angry with your Children, have an holy Anger with yourselves, and use this or the like Meditation with your own Souls, *Lord, shall I now punish my own Sin in mine own Child? Shall I now persecute the Corruptions of mine own Ancestor's? How then may I be displeased with me for the same carnal Conception of my own*

---

sacred writings, which are able to make you wise for salvation through faith in Christ Jesus." ESV.

[45] Job 4:6, 21 "Is not your fear of God your confidence, and the integrity of your ways your hope?", "Is not their tent-cord plucked up within them, do they not die, and that without wisdom?"

Child: It may be, I then lay in some Sin, or I asked it not of you by Prayer: Be merciful to me, O Lord; and in your good Time, show your pity on me and my Child!

    vi. As Children grow in Years, and in the Knowledge of Christ, let Parents train them up in the Exercise of all *Duties*, as *Prayer, Meditation, Self-Examination, Watchfulness, and all Means public and private*: If this be done, the World to come may reap the benefit of their Education; such Children as you bring up, such Parents will they be (when you are gone) to their Children; and such Children shall they have, who are Parents in the next Generation[46]. You are the very making or marring of the World: but on the contrary, if this be neglected. The rich Man will rise up against you in the Day of Judgement, and condemn you; for he being in Hell, had a Care of his Father's House, that they might be forewarned: he desired *Abraham to send Lazarus to his Brethren, to testify unto them that they came not to that Place of Torment*;[47] but you will not admonish your Children, you will not teach them *Moses and the Prophets*;[48] you will not show them the Dangers of God's heavy Displeasure hanging over their heads; you will not, while you live, lead a good Example before them: O you may fear that your Children shall be Furies of Hell to torment you. *Now the Lord open your Eyes to foresee, & to fly these judgments to come.*

3. The last Time to which the *Duty* of Parents extends itself, is the Time of their Departure out of their World; and then they owe their Children: Good Direction. & Faithful Prayer.

    a. For *Direction*: When Parents observe their Time to draw near, it is their Duty then especially, to commend some wise and wholesome Precepts unto their Children, the better to direct them in their Christian Course; so did *Isaac*, and *Jacob*, and *David*: The Words of a dying Parent are especially regarded, and make a deeper impression.

---

[46] As parents we are not just looking at our own children as the objects of our training, but also our grand-children and great-grand children . What we do now can have lasting spiritual benefits for generations to come.

[47] See the story told by Christ in Luke 16: 19-31.

[48] A phrase used by Abraham to the Rich Man to mean the whole of the scriptures.

b. For Prayer: then is the most proper Time for Parents to pray and to bless all their Children. As they commend their Souls unto God's Grace: God's *Providence and Promise are the best Inheritance in the World*; and if Parents (in their Prayers) leave these to their Children, they can never want any Thing that is good. O the faithful Prayers of Parents for their Children (especially when they are leaving their Children, and going to God) must needs, *in, for, and through Christ*, prevail mightily with God.

SECTION 4
OF THE DUTIES OF MASTERS TO SERVANTS

The *Duty* of *Masters* to their *Servants* is either to their Bodies, or to their Souls.

1. The *Duty* of *Masters* to the *Bodies* of their Servants, consists in these Particulars; *viz.* In a due Provision of Food for them, *Prov.* 31.15. and 27.27. In a wise Care for their Clothing, *Prov.* 31.21. In a well-ordering of their Labor, so as they may be able to undergo it: In their Ease, Rest, and Intermission from Labor at seasonable Times: In paying them sufficient Wages, *Deut.* 24.14. In a careful preserving of their Health, and using Means for their Recovery in Case of Sickness, *Mat.* 8.6. and that not of the Servants Wages, but of the Master's own Charge, otherwise they *undo not the heavy Burthen*[49], but rather lay Burthen upon Burthen.
2. The *Duty* of *Masters* to the *Souls* of their *Servants,* consist in these Particulars, *viz.* In teaching them the Principles of Religion, and all Duties of Piety: In causing them to go to the public Ministry of the Word and Worship of God: In taking an Account of their profiting by the public and private Means of Edification: In praying for them; and as they observe any Grace wrought in them, in praising God for it, and praying for the increase of it: Nothing so much wins a Servant's Heart, or the Affections of any gracious Heart, as the edifying of it in Grace.

---

[49] An archaic spelling of burden.

SECTION 5
OF THE DUTIES OF HUSBAND AND WIFE

THE Duties which the chief Governor and his Helper owe to one another, are either Common and mutual; or proper and peculiar to each severally:

1. The common mutual *Duties* between Man and Wife, are either Of Necessity to the being of Marriage; as *Matrimonial Unity;* or *Matrimonial Chastity:* Of Honesty to the well-being of Marriage; as a loving Affection of one another; Provident Care for one another. *Mat.* 19.6.[50] *Tit.* 2.5[51]. *Mal.* 2.15[52]. The former Duties presupposed: there ought to be—
    a. A sweet, loving, and tender-hearted pouring out of their Hearts, with much affectionate Dearness into one another's Bosoms. This mutual-melting-heartedness, being preserved fresh and fruitful, will infinitely sweeten and beautify the Marriage State. Now for the Preservation of

---

[50] "So they are no longer two but one flesh. What therefore God has joined together, let not man separate." ESV.

[51] "to be self-controlled, pure, working at home, kind, and submissive to their own husbands, that the word of God may not be reviled." ESV.

[52] "Did he not make them one, with a portion of the Spirit in their union? And what was the one God seeking? Godly offspring. So guard yourselves in your spirit, and let none of you be faithless to the wife of your youth." ESV.

this Love, let them consider.
  i. The compassionate and melting Compellations which Christ and his Spouse exchange in the *Canticles*, *My fair one, my Love, my Dove, my undefiled, my well-beloved, the chief of ten Thousand:* Such a fervent and chaste Love as this, all married Couples should resemble and imitate.
  ii. The Command of God to this Purpose, *Husbands love your Wives*, Eph. 5.25. and *Wives* (or young Women) *love your Husbands*, Tit. 2.4. Methinks this Charge often remembered, should ever beat back all Heart-rising and Bitterness, all wicked Wishes, that they had never met together, that they had never seen one another's Faces. When the Knot is tied, every Man should think his Wife the fittest for him, and every Wife should think her Husband the fittest for her of any other in the World.
 b. A provident Care of one for another; which extends to the Body: *No Man hateth his own Flesh, but nourisheth and cherisheth it:*[53] and to the good Name: *Joseph* was *not willing to make* Mary *a public Example:*[54] and to the Goods of this World; in which if there fall out any cross Providence, they are both to join with *Job's* Spirit, *The Lord hath given, and the Lord hath taken &c.*[55] But especially to the Soul; in praying together, for, and with one another: in taking Notice of the Beginning and least Measure of Grace, and approving the same; in conferring about such Things as concern the same, mutually propounding Questions, and giving Answers one to another; in maintaining holy and religious Exercises in the Family, and betwixt their own selves, in stirring up one another to hear the Word, to receive the Sacraments, and conscionably to perform all the Parts of God's public Worship: In case the one prove unconverted, let the other wait, and pray, and expect God's good Time: or in Case the one be a Babe in Christ, or weak in Christianity, let the other deal fairly, lovingly, meekly, and let our Lord Jesus his tender-heartedness to spiritual

---

[53] Ephesians 5:29.

[54] Matthew 1:19 "And her husband Joseph, being a just man and unwilling to put her to shame, resolved to divorce her quietly." ESV.

[55] Job 1:21.

Younglings, teach us Mercy this Way, who is said to *gather the Lambs with his Arms, and to carry them in his Bosom, and gently to lead those that are with young.*[56]

2. The proper and peculiar Duties to each severally, are—
    a. Of the Husband, whose *Duty* it is, 1. That he dearly love his Wife. 2. That he wisely maintain and manage his Authority over her.
        i. For the former, 1. *The Matter of it* is a dear Love, a special Love, and a more special then that common mutual Love to one another: No question the Wife is to love her Husband, and a Brother to love his Brother, and a Friend to love his Friend; but more especially, or with a more *special Love*, is the Husband to love his Wife. To this Purpose she is called, *The Wife of his Bosom*,[57] to shew, that she ought to be as his *Heart* in his Bosom. He must love her at all Times, he must love her in all Things: Love must season and sweeten his Speech, Carriage, and Actions towards her: Love must shew itself in his Commands, Reproofs, Admonitions, Instructions, Authority, Familiarity with her, the Rise of which Love must not be from her Beauty, Nobility, or because she contents and pleases her Husband; but especially because she is his Sister in the Profession of Christian Religion, and an Inheritor with him of the Kingdom of Heaven: because of her Graces, and Virtues, as Modesty, Chastity, Diligence, Patience, Temperance, Faithfulness, Secrecy, Obedience, &c. because she bears and brings him forth Children, the Heirs of his Name and Substance, and the Upholder of his Family; and because of the Union and Conjunction of Marriage. Love growing on Beauty, Riches, Lust, or any other slight Grounds, is but a Blaze, and soon vanished, but if grounded on these Considerations, and especially on this Union of Marriage, it is lasting and true: The want hereof is the Fountain of Strife, Quarrelling, Debate; which converts the Paradise of Marriage, into an Hell.
            1. For the *manner of this Love;* the Apostle gives it thus, *Husbands love your own Wives even as Christ also*

---

[56] Isaiah 40:11.

[57] Deuteronomy 28:54.

loved the Church. Now the Love of Christ to his Church, is commended to us in these Particulars: —

    a. In *the Case of his Love,* which is his *Love: He set his Love on you, because he loved you:* [58]his Love arose wholly and solely from himself, and was every Way free: so should Husbands love their Wives, tho' there be nothing in Wives to move them, but merely because they are Wives.

    b. In *the Order of his Love:* Christ began it to the Church, before the Church could love him: And as a Wall is first smitten on by the Sun-beams, before it give a Reflection of her Heat back again: so the Church is first heated and warmed at Heart by the Sense of Christ's Love, before she love him again: *We love him, because he loved us first:*[59] — *Because of the Savour of thy Ointments, therefore do the Virgins love thee:*[60] So should Husbands begin to love their own Wives. I know some Wives prevent their Husbands herein, and there may be Reason for it; but the greater is their Glory. This Pattern of Christ should rather stir up the Husbands to go before them.

    c. In *the Truth of Christ's Love:* This was manifested by the Fruits thereof to his Church: *He gave himself for it, that he might sanctify it, & cleanse it, & present it to himself a glorious Church, not having spot or wrinkle:*[61] So must Husbands *love* their Wives in Truth and indeed, by guiding them in the Way of Life, and Path that is *holy;* for this is the truest Character of a sincere Love.

    d. In *the Quality of his Love:* Christ's *Love* is an holy,

---

[58] Deuteronomy 7:7 "It was not because you were more in number than any other people that the LORD set his love on you and chose you, for you were the fewest of all peoples," ESV.

[59] 1 John 4:19.

[60] Song of Solomon 1:3.

[61] Ephesians 5:27.

pure, and chaste *Love;* as he himself is, so is his *Love;* such must be the *love* of Husbands, an holy, pure, and chaste *Love.* Away with all intemperate, excessive, or any Ways exorbitant Pollutions of the Marriage-Bed! from which, if the fear of God, imitation of Christ, love of Purity, awfulness of God's all-seeing Eye cannot draw, yet that slavish Horror, lest God should punish such a Couple with no Children, or with misshapen Children, or with Idiots, or with prodigious wicked Children, or with some other heavy Cross; one would think should be able to affright them.

 e. In *the Continuance of Christ's Love? Having loved his own, he loved them to the End.*[62] His *Love* is a constant *Love,* an everlasting *Love.* No Provocation or Transgressions could ever make him forget his *Love. Thou hast played the Harlot with many Lovers, yet return unto me.* Jer. 3.1. Such must be the Love of Husbands, affirm *Love,* an inviolable *Love:* The Ground of it must be God's Ordinance, and the Support of it must be an inviolable Resolution, that no Provocation shall ever change or alter it. Husbands must pass by all Infirmities, endeavoring in Love to redress them, if possibly they can; or if not, to bear with them.

ii. Duty of an Husband, is, *wisely to maintain and manage his Authority.* Now the managing of it consists in two Things: 1. That he tenderly respect her. 2. That he carefully provide for her.

 1. He must *tenderly respect her,* as his Wife, Companion, Yoke-fellow, as his very Delight; and the *Desire of his Eyes,* and *never be bitter against her.*[63] This Bitterness ordinarily turn the Edge of his Authority. If therefore any Matter of Unkindness arise (as sometimes certainly will) then must he carefully with all Lenity, Gentleness and Patience quiet all, and

---

[62] John 13:1.

[63] Colossians 3:19.

never suffer himself nor his Wife to sleep in Displeasure: *Let not the Sun go down upon your Wrath,*[64] or if he shall have Occasion to reprove her, he must keep his Words until a convenient time, and not do it in Presence of others; and then utter them in the Spirit of Meekness and Love. Surely if she be not corrected by a Word of Wisdom and Discretion, she will never amend by Threats, or any hasty, rigorous Carriage: and if she once begin to lose her Shamefacedness in the Presence of her Husband, it is likely there will be often Brawling and Quarrelling betwixt them, and the House will be full of Disquietness: It is best therefore to deal wisely with her, to admonish her often, to reprehend her seldom, never to lay violent Hands on her; and if she be dutiful, to cherish her, that she may so continue; if wayward, mildly to suffer her, that she wax not worse.

2. He must *carefully provide for her:* To this purpose he is called her Head, and Savior, as *Christ is the Head of his Church,*[65] and the Savior of the Body: The *Head* (you know) is the Fountain of Motion, Quickening, Life, Sense, and Lightsomeness to the body; so should the Husband be as the Well-spring of Liveliness, Lightsomeness, Light heartedness to his Wife; she hath forsook all for him, and therefore she should receive from him a continual Influence of cheerful Walking, and comfortable enjoying of herself. And a *Savior* (you know) both provides for, and protects the saved: Christ thus saved his Church; he is every Way a sufficient Savior, *able perfectly to save, even to the very uttermost,*[66] he saves Soul and Body, he saves from all Manner of Misery, from the Wrath of God, the Curse of the Law, the Venom of all outward Crosses, the Tyranny of Satan, the Sting of Death, the Power of the Grave, the Torments of Hell; or, if

---

[64] Ephesians 4:26.

[65] Ephesians 5:23.

[66] Hebrews 7:25.

Sin be the greatest Evil, (as indeed it is) *he will save his People from their Sins;* Mat. 1.21. I cannot say thus of the Husband; yet an Husband carried a Resemblance of Christ, and is after a Manner a *Savior* to his Wife, to protect her and to provide for her. *David* compares her to a *Vine*,[67] intimating that as a *Vine* is underpropped and raised by some Tree or Frame near to which it is planted; so is the Wife raised to the Height of Honor by Virtue of her Relation to her Husband; by his Wealth she is enriched; by his Honor she is dignified: he is under God and Christ, *all in all to her.* In the Family, he is a King, to govern and aid her; a Priest, to pray with her and for her; a Prophet, to teach and instruct her; a *Savior* to provide for, and protect her to *his utmost,* if not to *the utmost;* which indeed is proper and peculiar to the Lord Jesus Christ.

3. The Duties proper to the Wife, are these, *viz.* 1. That she be in Submission to her Husband. 2. That she be an Helper to him all her Days.

   a. *Wives must he in subjection to their own Husbands: Sarah obeyed Abraham, and called him Lord:* Gen. 3.16. Eph. 5.22. 1 Pet. 3.16. But here is a Case of Conscience,—

      i. What if her Husband be a Son of *Belial,* an Enemy to Christ? Must she then yield Subjection?— Yes: because in his Office her Husband is as in Christ Stead: The Church is compared to *a Lilly among Thorns,* she remains *Lilly-like;* white, soft, pleasant, and amiable, tho' she be joined with *Thorns,* which are prickly and sharp: So a Wife must be meek, mild, gentle, obedient, tho' she be matched with a crooked, perverse, profane and wicked Husband: She must in this Case remove her Eyes from the Disposition of her Husband's Person, to the Condition of his Place; and by Virtue thereof (seeing he bears Christ's Image) be subject unto him as unto Christ.

      ii. What if her Husband command Things contrary to Christ? Must she therein be subject? — No: *Submit,*

---

[67] Ambrose may be referencing Psalm 128:4, "Your wife will be like a fruitful vine within your house; your children will be like olive shoots around your table." ESV However the author of this Psalm is not known.

&c. How? *as unto the Lord*: if she submits to Things contrary to Christ, she submits not *as to the Lord*. Conscientious Wives must remember, they have an Husband in Heaven, as well as on Earth, between whom there is a greater difference, than between Heaven and Earth; and therefore in Case they bid contrary Things, they must prefer God before Man, Christ before all Men.[68]

b. *Wives must be helpers to their Husbands.* Now this Helpfulness consists in these Things:

i. That she be careful to preserve his Person, in Sickness or in Health, in Adversity, or Prosperity, in Youth or old Age. A most memorable and famous Pattern for this Purpose, is recorded by *Uves*:[69] *A young, tender, and beautiful Maid; was matched to a Man stricken in Years, whom after Marriage she found to have a very diseased Body, full of loathful Diseases: yet notwithstanding, out of Sense and Conscience, that by God's Providence she was become his Wife, she most worthily digested all with incredible Patience: Friends and Physicians advised her by no Means to come near him; and for their Parts, they utterly forsook him; but she (passing by with a loving Disdain those unkind Dissuasions) becomes to him in their Stead, Friend, Physician, Nurse, Mother, Sister, Daughter, Servant, every Thing, any Thing to do him Good any manner of way. At last by extraordinary Expense, and excessive Charges about him, she came to some want of some Necessaries; whereupon she sold her Rings, Chains, richest Attire, Plate, and choicest Jewels: and when he was dead, and Friends came about her, rather*

---

[68] Ambrose provides the biblical balance inherent in the submission that is the holy calling of wives; *Wives must remember, they have an Husband in Heaven, as well as on Earth*. This can be a very difficult matter and not taken lightly for those wives finding themselves under ungodly husbands. It is Christ who gives the wife this holy calling and it is Christ that she must bind herself to before her husband. Obedience to her husband is obedience to Christ foremost. Therefore, it is not a calling of submission to endure such things as physical abuse, as some have suggested at times, because this is wholly contrary to the nature of her heavenly husband.

[69] Not much is known about this work. Ambrose cites it as *Lib. 2. de Christiana faem. p. 360*. The English title of this work would be *The Virgin Christiana*.

to congratulate her happy Riddance, than to bewail her Widowhood; she not only abhorred all Speeches tending that Way, but protested, if it were possible, she would willingly redeem her Husband's Life with the loss of her five dearest Children. Whence it appears that this worthy Woman was wedded to her Husband's Soul, not to his Body; seeing no Infirmity or Deformity thereof, could cool or weaken the fervency of her Love.

ii. That she learn and labor to forecast, contrive and manage Household Affairs, and *Business within Doors*, as they say: for which see a right noble glorious Pattern in *Prov.* 31.

iii. That she help her Husband, in setting forward the rich and royal Trade of Grace, in erecting and establishing Christ's glorious Kingdom in their House, and especially in their own Hearts. This is that *one necessary Thing,* without which their Family is but Satan's Seminary, and a Nursery for Hell: This will marvelously sweeten all Reproaches, cast upon them by envenomed Tongues: This will sweetly seal unto them their Assurance of meeting together hereafter in Heaven,— Where the Husband and Wife perform these and the like *Duties;* there's an happy Family, there's a College of Quietness; where these are neglected, we may term it an Hell,

Thus much of the *Duties* of Governors; we now come to the Governed.

SECTION 6
OF THE DUTIES OF CHILDREN TO PARENTS

Duties of Children to Parents, are either inward, as *Love and Fear;* or outward, as *Reverence, Obedience,* and *Recompense.*
1. The inward *Duties* which Children owe to their Parents, are *Love and Fear: Love* like Sugar, sweetens *Fear,* and *Fear* like Salt, seasons *Love;* there must be a loving Fear, and a fearing Love. Hence the *Fear* of a Child is opposed to the *Fear* of a Slave; for a Child's *Fear* being mixed with *Love,* has respect to the Office which a Parent may take: But a Slaves *Fear,* which is ordinarily mixed with Hatred, has respect to nothing but the Punishment which his Master may inflict upon him. This *love-like Fear* is so proper to Children, as that the awful Respect which the Saints bear to God, is called *a filial Fear*[70]; Children have received their Substance, from the very Substance of their Parents, and therefore they are to perform this *Duty* of *Love* and *Fear* to them.
2. The outward *Duties,* or the Manifestation of this *Love* and *Fear* in Children, appears;
    a. In their Reverence, *in Speech and Carriage:* They must give to their Parents reverent and honorable Titles, meek and humble Speeches, Obedience, as becomes their Age and Sex: Thus *Joseph* and *Solomon* bowed, the one to his Father,

---

[70] Filial is a duty owed by a son or daughter to a parent as in a display of filial affection. As used here it would represent a love that would dread or fear offending the parent.

the other to his Mother, *Gen.* 48.12.[71] 1 *Kin.* 2.19.[72] Contrary hereto is mocking and despising Father and Mother: of which, said *Solomon*, *The Eye that mocketh at his Father, and despiseth to obey his Mother, the Ravens of the Valley shall pick it out;* Prov. 13.17.[73] A Phrase that sets forth the End of a notorious Malefactor, that is hanged in the Air till the Ravens pick out his Eyes.

    b. In their Obedience to their Commands, Instructions, Reproofs and Corrections of their Parents, *Eph.* 6.1.[74] *Prov.* 1.8, 9[75]. The Reason is, because of God, whom the Father represents: Children must remember, that whatever they do to their Parents, they do it to God; when they please them, they please God; when their Parents are justly angry with them, God is angry with them: nor can they recover God's Favor (tho' all the Saints of Heaven should entreat for them) till they have submitted themselves to their own Parents; only with this Limitation, that they submit or obey them *in the Lord,* Eph. 6.1.

    c. In their Recompense: This is a *Duty* whereby Children endeavor (as much as in them lies) to repay what they can for the Parents Kindness, Care and Cost towards them, in way of Thankfulness: *If any Widow have Children, or Nephews, let them first learn to shew Kindness at Home, and to requite their*

---

[71] "And Joseph brought them out from between his knees, and he bowed himself with his face to the earth." KJV.

[72] "Bathsheba therefore went unto king Solomon, to speak unto him for Adonijah. And the king rose up to meet her, and bowed himself unto her, and sat down on his throne, and caused a seat to be set for the king's mother; and she sat on his right hand." KJV.

[73] The quotation is actually Proverbs 30:17. Ambrose cites Proverbs 13:17 which is meant to be an additional reference and not the location of the cited text. Proverbs 13:17 reads, "A wicked messenger falls into trouble, but a faithful envoy brings healing." ESV.

[74] "Children, obey your parents in the Lord: for this is right." KJV.

[75] "Hear, my son, your father's instruction, and forsake not your mother's teaching, for they are a graceful garland for your head and pendants for your neck." ESV.

Parents, 1 Tim. 5.4. In Sickness, they must visit them, in the time of Mourning, they must comfort them; in Want, they must provide for them: As the Children of *Jacob,* who visited, comforted, and went to buy Food for their Father, *Gen.* 48.1. & 37.35. & 42.3.[76] In time of Danger, they must endeavor their Protection; as *David* did, 1 Sam. 22.3, 4. *Let my Father and Mother* (said he to the King of *Moab*) *I pray thee, come forth and be with you, till I know what God will do for me: And he brought them before the King of Moab, and they dwelt with him all the while that David was in the hold.*

If God please to take Children out of this World before their Parents, and their Parents be succourless,[77] they must (as they can) provide for their well-being after their Deaths: Thus Christ commended his Mother to his Disciple *John,* a little before he gave up the Ghost.[78] It is recorded of the Stork, that when the Dams are old, the young Ones feed them; and when thro' Age they are ready to faint in their flying, the young Ones help them; and when they are past flying, the young Ones carry them on their weak Backs. Thus Nature teaches Children their Duty, how much more should Grace.?

---

[76] "And it came to pass after these things, that *one* told Joseph, Behold, thy father *is* sick: and he took with him his two sons, Manasseh and Ephraim." "And all his sons and all his daughters rose up to comfort him; but he refused to be comforted; and he said, For I will go down into the grave unto my son mourning. Thus his father wept for him." "And Joseph's ten brethren went down to buy corn in Egypt." KJV.

[77] To be helpless.

[78] John 19:26-27

SECTION 7
OF THE DUTIES OF SERVANTS TO THEIR MASTERS

Duties of Servants to their Masters, are either inward, as *Fear*, outward, as *Reverence, Obedience*.[79]

1. The inward *Duty* is *Fear: Servants be subject to your Masters with all Fear, and account them worthy of all Honor:*[80] So proper is this Fear to a Servant, as where it is wanting, there is a plain denial of his Master's Place and Power: *If I be a Master, where is my Fear?* said God. Observe, I mean not an excessive slavish Fear; as when a Servant fears nothing but the revenging Power of his Master (such was the Fear of that unprofitable Servant, who could say to his Master, *I knew that thou wert an hard Man, and I was afraid*)[81] but I mean an awful Fear of Provoking his Master's Wrath, so as it makes him cast every Way, how he may please his Master, and such a Fear draws him on cheerfully to perform his *Duty*.
2. Outward Duties which issue from this Fear, are *Reverence, Obedience*.
    a. *Reverence*, which is manifested in Speech & Carriage. Thus

---

[79] At first glance this section may seem rooted in a time past and of no relevance today. But as employees under an owner we should step back and soak in what Ambrose says here regarding servants, since in an *at will* condition, we do serve a master.

[80] A variant of 1 Peter 2:18.

[81] Matthew 25:24.

Servants must give reverend Titles to their Masters, as *Father*, *Lord*, and *Master*, *&c.* They must yield Obeisance[82] to them; as *The Children of the Prophets, when they saw that the Spirit of Elijah rested on Elisha, they came to meet him, and bowed themselves to the Ground before him.*[83]

b. *Obedience;* which has Respect to the Commands, Instructions, Reproofs & Corrections of their Masters, 1 *Pet.* 2.18, 19, 20. But here's a Case or two of Conscience:

i. How far they must obey; or what is the extent of Servants Obedience to Masters? — The Apostle answers, *Servants obey in all Things your Masters according to the Flesh,* Col. 3.22. It is not sufficient that Servants perform well their *Duties* in some Things; they must do it in *all Things;* yea in Things that may be against their own Mind and Liking, if their Masters will have it so: This is clear in the Example of *Joab, the King commands him to number the People: Joab* declares himself, that he thinks it a very unmeet Thing. *Why doth my Lord the King delight* (saith he) *in this Thing?* 2 Sam. 24.2, &c. Yet against his Judgment he yields unto the King's peremptory[84] Command, *The King's Word prevailed against Joab.* Look as *Peter,* when Christ bid him launch out into the Deep, and let down his Net for a Draught, *He answered and said, Master, We have toiled all the Night, and have taken nothing: nevertheless at thy Word, I will let down the Net.*[85] So must Servants say, when they have a peremptory Command, tho' contrary to their own Judgments, this or that in all Humility, I suppose, or I propound to you; *Nevertheless, at your Word I will let down the Net;* I will do as you please.

ii. But what if God and Master should command contrary

---

[82] An older term that means to show a high regard of respect. Typically as an outward action like a bow or curtsy. The connection is typically with paying respect to a high official or royalty. Today this term is employed by Jehovah Witnesses to circumvent the clear worship of Christ as God the Son by the disciples in the New Testament.

[83] 2 Kings 2:15.

[84] An instance on immediate obedience given in a harsh manner.

[85] Luke 5:5.

Things? In such a Case the Apostle sets down an excellent Limitation in these four Phrases, [1. *As unto Christ.* 2. *As the Servants of Christ.* 3. *Doing the Will of God.* 4. *As to the Lord.*] All these imply, That if Masters command their Servants any Thing contrary to Christ, they may not yield to it:[86] Upon this Ground the Midwives of the Hebrew Women, would not kill the *Hebrew* Children, *They feared God* (saith the Text) *and did not as the King commanded them*, Exod. 1.17. In this Case, *Joseph* is commended, in not hearkening to his Mistress[87]; and the Servants of *Saul* are commended, for refusing to slay the Lord's Priests[88], at their Masters Command. When Masters Command or forbid any Thing against God & Christ, they go therein beyond their Commission, and their Authority ceases; so that Servants may say, *We ought to obey God rather than Men*, Act. 5.29.

3. *Objection*[89]. But some may object, *That all Men are alike, and that there is no Difference as between Masters and Servants; nay, it is expressly forbidden to be Servants of Men.* 1 Cor. 7.23.[90]

   a. I answer, To *be a Servant*, in that Place, is not simply to be in Subjection under another, but to be so obsequious[91] to Man, as to prefer him before *God:* Hence the Apostle elsewhere in the *Duties* of Servants, lays down this Antithesis, *Not as Men-pleasers, but as the Servants of Christ;* again, *doing Service as to the Lord, and not to Men:* The meaning is, That we must do *Duty* to a *Master*, not as merely to a *Man*, but as to one *in Christ's Stead.* Masters, by

---

[86] This is extremely relevant to employees at this time, especially lower magistrates (government officials) as we are asked to perform tasks that are contrary to God definition of marriage; as one example.

[87] Genesis 39:12.

[88] 1 Samuel 22:17.

[89] Ambrose labeled this as item 5. It has been re-labeled as section 3 to continue the proper flow.

[90] "You were bought with a price; do not become bondservants of men." ESV.

[91] To be serving in such a capacity that you doing so to an excessive degree.

virtue of their Office and Place, bear the Image of Christ; Christ communicates his Authority unto them, and so in performing *Duty* to Masters, we perform *Duty* to Christ, and in denying *Duty* to Masters, we deny *Duty* to Christ: Thus the Lord said to *Samuel,* when the People rejected his Government, *They have not rejected thee, but they have rejected me, that I should not reign over them.*[92] Consider this, all ye that are *Servants,* though *Masters* should neither reward your good Service, nor revenge your ill Service, yet Christ will do both: This is your Prerogative that fear God, above all other Servants; others may serve their Masters with *Fear and Trembling,* in Singleness of Heart, and with good Will, but only Christians and Saints do *Service as to Christ;* and this makes them not content themselves with doing the Thing, but to endeavor to do it after the best Manner they can, so as God and Christ may accept of it.

I have now run thro' the Family, and informed you of the *Duties* both of *Governors* and *Governed.* Christians, look within you, look about you: *That Man is not a good Man, that is not good in all his Relations.* The same God that requires us to serve him as private Persons, requires us to serve him in our Relations: And therefore, though you be never so careful of your *Duty* in the former Respect, yet you may go to Hell for neglecting your *Duties,* as *Masters, Servants, Husbands, Wives, Parents,* or *Children:* Nay, I'll say a little more, that though you should be good in one Relation, yet if you endeavor not to be good in every Relation, you shall never go to Heaven:[93] for the same God that commands you to serve him as a Master, commands you to serve him as a Father, as an Husband, &c. *And he that keeps the whole Law, and offends in one Point, is guilty of all,* Jam. 2.10.

---

[92] 1 Samuel 8:7.

[93] Do not misunderstand what Ambrose is saying. He is not saying that salvation is based in works. No, it is through Christ alone, by grace alone, and faith alone. Rather, if you have no love to obey Christ in these matters then you should examine yourself to see if you are even in the faith. For those who are in Christ, love Christ, and strive to obey Christ in all things.

ISAAC AMBROSE

A BIOGRAPHICAL SKETCH

Born in 1604 under the rule of James I, Isaac Ambrose lived during a politically and spiritually unsettled time through most of the 17th century. His father was Richard Ambrose, the Vicar of Ormskirk and while much is not known about Isaac's childhood, there must have been some influence of his father leading him to study for the pastorate in 1621 at Brasenose at the age of 17. He completed his studies in 1625 with his BA and his masters from Trinity College; this no doubt gave him the depth and background he later drew from in his preaching.

Being ordained Ambrose became the Vicar of Castleton. He referred to the position as the "little cure" in which he served from June 17th, 1627 to 1631. This vicarage still stand today as you can see behind me. After this, he served as Vicar in Yorkshire. It was during this time that Isaac, through the influence of the Earl of Bedford, became one of four itinerate preachers of under the King, a prestigious position that he held officially until April 12th, 1662. The King's Itinerant preachers were originally formed to convert the Catholics to Protestantism, but now had a less reforming nature about it. As an itinerate preacher Isaac was stationed at Garstang, 10 miles north of Preston in Lancashire.

Ambrose's ability as a preacher was becoming well known. At some point, he caught the ear of Lady Margaret Hoghton, known as the "Patroness of godly preachers" and she convinced him to leave Garstang and become the vicar of Preston in 1639. Isaac developed a close relationship with her family. In 1654 Isaac returned to Garstang because the vicarage had been left vacant. This appointment was to the reluctance of Isaac and the disappointment of the Lady Margaret. This relationship is seen in Ambrose's sermon, "Redeeming the Time" preached at her funeral on January 4th, 1657. Here he said, "the Lord made her the first wheel of his providence in bringing me hither, and it was some trouble to her spirit, that I left this Pastoral change before she left the world."

Ambrose remained at Garstang until 1662 until removed under the Bartholomew Act for refusing to make the required declaration.

Now something needs to be said about the political and religious atmosphere of the day and Ambrose's involvement to understand him as a person. When Ambrose entered the ministry under the reign of Charles I there was an atmosphere of distrust that grew as time went on. Charles' I marriage to Henrietta Maria of France, a Roman Catholic did not help matters. This turbulence eventually erupted into civil war in 1642 between the King and the Parliamentarian forces of Oliver Cromwell. With the defeat of the royalist in 1646 the parliament enacted new laws regarding religious freedom. In October of that year, the Anglican Episcopacy was abolished. Ambrose had no issues accepting the new Presbyterian form of government. This new form of government created classes of which Ambrose's name appears in the seventh of his county. These comprised of the most ardent Presbyterian leaders of the day, and he played a prominent part in the provincial assembly that met in Preston; often serving a moderator of its meetings. In 1648, Ambrose was one of the signatories of a document called the "Harmonious Consent" which voiced support of the Westminster Assembly and also a document known as "the Agreement of the People taken into consideration" that gave a negative review of an official paper urging constitutional changes. This latter action landed Ambrose in prison for a short time. Not his first imprisonment; 1642 and 43 landed him in jail under the Kings commissioner of array for refusing to support the Royalist cause. However, each time Ambrose's influential friends were able to garner his release in short order.

With the return of King Charles II after the collapse of the Commonwealth, persecution increased. In 1662, there was a gathering of twenty ministers to discuss how they would handle the new directives of the King under the uniformity act that reestablished the Anglican Church government. At this meeting, Ambrose stated he would use the Common Book of Prayer, and most agreed with him. However, this was not enough to keep him and the others from being ejected by the king and listed among the 2,000 ministers ejected or silenced in the Nonconformist Memorial.

Ambrose had a family life as well, but not well documented. He married his wife Judith who gave him three children; Richard, Augustine, and Rachel. Ambrose resided to solitude in his last days, spending time in meditation and writing. After his death in 1664, his wife lived with their daughter until she died a few years later.

AMBROSE PIETY

From his work entitled *Looking unto Jesus*, Ambrose writes, "Oh! How should all hearts be taken with this Christ? Christians! Turn your eyes upon the Lord: 'Look, and look again unto Jesus.' Why stand ye gazing on the toys of this world, when such a Christ is offered to you in the gospel? Can the world die for you? Can the world reconcile you top the father? Can the world advance you to the kingdom of heaven? As Christ is all in all, so let him be the full and complete subject of our desire, and hope, and faith, and love, and joy: let him be in your thoughts the first in the morning, and the last at night."
While Ambrose lived through divisive and troublesome times, he was known for his gentleness and devotion to his flock. One person quoted said, "he was holy in life, happy in his death, honored by God, and held in high estimation by all good men."

A Life of Solitude in Meditation

One theme that plowed through Ambrose's life, both private and publicly, is his emphasis on a life of meditation on the things of God. "Let him be in your thought." This practice is in his life, his instruction, and his writings.
Those who were familiar with Ambrose knew of his habit of solitude in spiritual retreat. Having been taken under the care of Lady Hoghton afforded Ambrose the opportunity to retreat into the woods of Hoghton Tower, to a small hut in the woods for the span of a month during mid-May through June. He practiced this yearly. Ambrose describes this experience in a journal entry:

"I came to [the woods], which I did upon mature resolution, every year about that pleasant spring time (if the Lord pleased) to retire myself, and in some solitary and silent place to practice especially the secret duties of a Christian: In this place are sweet silent woods, and therein this month, and part of the next, the Lord by his Spirit wrought in me evangelical repentance for sin, gave me sweet comforts, and spiritual refreshings in my commerce and intercourse with him, by prayer, and meditation, and self-examination, and discovered to me the causes of my many troubles and discouragements in my ministry"

No doubt many of his sermons and books are the fruit of this work of solitude and quiet meditation. Ambrose was able to focus on developing an intimacy with Christ without interruption. The idea of leaving the worries of the world for an entire month seems an impossible dream in a modern 21st-century busy life. But as we just saw, Ambrose lived a full life as a pastor, an intenerate preacher, writer, and served in many capacities within the religious structure and his community; let alone raising a family and being a husband. He developed a discipline about this that we would do well to learn.

This time of meditation he patterned after our patriarch Isaac in Genesis 24:63, which reads, "And he went out to meditate in the field toward evening." Likewise, Isaac Ambrose would depart into creation for a time to allow himself time with Christ.

INSTRUCTION TO CHRISTIANS IN MEDITATION

Ambrose did not just practice this meditation but also instructed his flock and encouraged Christians to take part. Ambrose defined mediation as a "deep and earnest mulling upon some point of Christian instruction, to strengthen us against the flesh, world and devil, and to the leading us forward towards the kingdom of heaven" He classified this into two types of meditation; sudden and deliberate. Sudden being a thing that God offers to us in His providence. On the other hand, on deliberate meditation he says, "is when we purposefully separate ourselves from all company, and go apart to perform this exercise more thoroughly, making choice of such matter, time and place as are most suited for it."

As an aid to Christians, Ambrose stresses that the Christian should be recording their time with Christ. In his work, Prima, Media, and Ultima, written in 1650 Ambrose encourages Christian in the discipline of journal keeping. Here he gives some examples for our benefit from his journal which has long disappeared. For example on May 17th he writes:
"This day in the morning I meditated on the Love of Christ, wherein Christ appeared, and melted my heart in many sweet passages. In the evening I meditated on eternity, wherein the Lord both melted, and cheered and warmed, and refreshed my soul."

The importance of journaling and meditation is illustrated further in the Christian Warrior where Ambrose says, "Many saints of God have reaped no small benefit by recording the dealings of God with their own souls, and looking over them in times of distress." He goes on the relay a story of a woman who sank into depression until reading her diary and meditating on the past loving-kindness of the Lord recorded there. In his diary Ambrose writes, "In evening I perused my diary from the last year, wherein [there was] many passages of mercies from God."

Ambrose laid out this practice of meditation in the following ways. He described entering into meditation either through prayer or theme. The prayer being short put very full, in which the Holy Spirit would direct the believer, and the theme is a topic or scripture selected by choice. The Christian then would continue towards an understanding of the scripture or theme through study and meditation ultimately ending in affection; an affection for Christ. Using this form of meditation gives the Christian a thankful heart lifted up to God and filled with sweetness and spiritual contentment.

Ambrose would extol his hearer to the importance of this Christian practice saying, "If you neglect the word, prayer, and meditation, it is folly to talk of your desires of [Christ]."

Expressed in His Writings

A desire for Christ is Ambrose focus in meditation and reflected in his writings. Mostly devotional in nature, they tend to provide instruction into the "secret duties of the Christian" The Christian Warrior acts as a manual for the Christian soldier to deal with sin, Satan, the world, and the flesh. Looking unto Jesus focuses on meditating on Christ from his first coming, his birth, life, death, and resurrection. Other works include *The practice of sanctification, Of self-denial, Of the life of Faith* and *Of Family Duties* which all have a familiar personal focus on duties rather than being deep theological treaties. This is not to say they do not dive deeply into the things of God.
In his book, *Of the Nature and Kinds of Meditation* he gives us examples of themes to meditate on. One example says, "Upon sight of the morning sky, meditate, that if one sun make so bright a morning what a shining morning will that be, when Christ the son of righteousness shall appear."

Another example for an evening time, Ambrose says, "Upon night approaching, meditate that seeing our days are determined, and the number of our months are with the Lord, and our bounds are appointed which we cannot pass that one day more of our limited time is gone and past, and we are now nearer to our end by a day, than we were in the morning."

Like a true shepherd, Ambrose kindly instructs with examples, illustrations, and the living out of his life. His writings are much like a father to a son providing instruction based on experience rather than theory. But to what end are we to follow his instruction?

Ambrose provides us with that answer in his work *The Practice of Sanctification* as he clearly explains the use and purpose of the duty of Meditation and its relationship with the Holy Spirit:

"I deny not, that if any should so think to work out his comforts by meditation, prayer, reading the word, as to attempt the work in his strength, and do not all in subordination to God, and the Spirit's assistance, the comfort will be nothing but vanity."

He goes on to say that the end in mind of this and all Christian duties are that the Lord Christ may be exalted. The main end of duties is the glory of him who hath redeemed us with the price of his blood."

So as we leave this time of study into the life of Isaac Ambrose, let me leave us with his words from his sermon, Redeeming the Time.

"It is but a while that you have to live, and therefore I beseech you improve time, lay hold of every season to get heaven. Live everyday as if it were your last on earth. Walk accurately, exactly, circumspectly, not as fools, but as wise, redeeming the time, because the days are evil"